LEARN ABOUT
TORNADOES

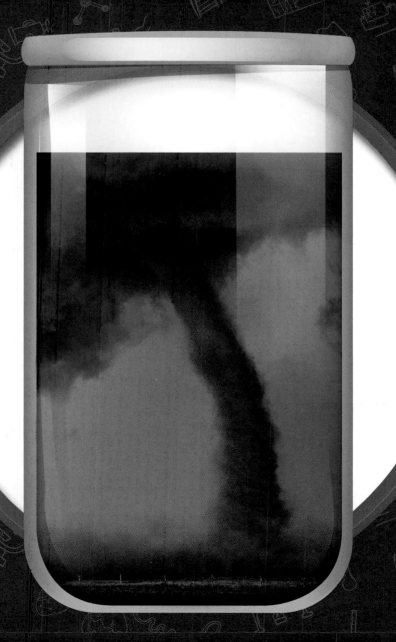

by Golriz Golkar

The Child's World®
childsworld.com

Published by The Child's World®
1980 Lookout Drive • Mankato, MN 56003-1705
800-599-READ • www.childsworld.com

Design Elements: Shutterstock Images
Photographs ©: Minerva Studio/Shutterstock Images, cover
(tornado), 1 (tornado), 11, 17; Shutterstock Images, cover (jar),
1 (jar), 4 (vinegar), 12, 18, 23; iStockphoto, 4 (soap); Elizabeth
A. Cummings/Shutterstock Images, 4 (food coloring); Rick
Orndorf, 5; Justin Hobson/Shutterstock Images, 6; Patrick
Heagney/iStockphoto, 9; Todd Shoemake/Shutterstock Images,
14; Alexey Stiop/Shutterstock Images, 20

ISBN 9781503832152
LCCN 2018962838

Printed in the United States of America
PA02420

About the Author

Golriz Golkar is a teacher and
children's author who lives
in Nice, France. She enjoys
cooking, traveling, and looking
for ladybugs on nature walks.

TABLE OF CONTENTS

CHAPTER 1

Let's Make a Tornado!

MATERIALS

- ☐ Glass jar with lid
- ☐ Water
- ☐ One teaspoon clear dish detergent
- ☐ Blue food coloring
- ☐ One teaspoon vinegar

It is a good idea to gather your materials before you begin.

A tornado forms in the water
when you swirl the jar!

STEPS

1. Fill $^3/_4$ of the jar with water.

2. Add the dish detergent. Add one drop
   of food coloring. Do not mix.

Tornadoes are known for their powerful winds.

3. Add the vinegar.

4. Close the jar lid tightly.

5. Hold the jar firmly by the lid. Rotate it quickly. Swirl the ingredients together. This forms a funnel shape. It looks like a tornado has formed!

CHAPTER 2

What Is a Tornado?

A tornado is a rotating air column. It is a powerful storm. It is sometimes called a twister. It has a twisting funnel. It reaches down from a thunderstorm to the ground. In the experiment, a funnel is created when the liquids swirl together.

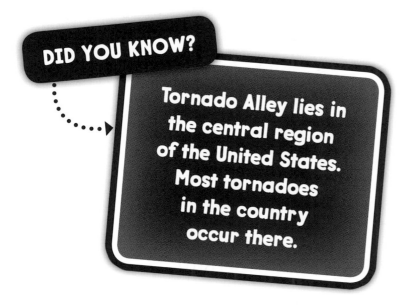

DID YOU KNOW?

Tornado Alley lies in the central region of the United States. Most tornadoes in the country occur there.

The powerful winds of tornadoes look like a swirling funnel.

Tornadoes occur around the world. Most happen in the United States. More than 1,000 form there each year. A tornado may last a few seconds. Others last up to three hours. A tornado's average speed is 30 miles (48 km) per hour. It rarely travels farther than six miles (10 km).

CHAPTER 3

What Happens During a Tornado?

Most tornadoes occur in spring and summer. They can happen any time of day. A tornado forms when warm, **humid** air interacts with cold, dry air. The **atmosphere** is usually warm. The ground is warm as well. The **dense** cold air moves above the warm air. Thunderstorms often begin in these conditions.

A tornado is likely to form when clouds begin to rotate.

The tornado travels downward from the thunderstorm.

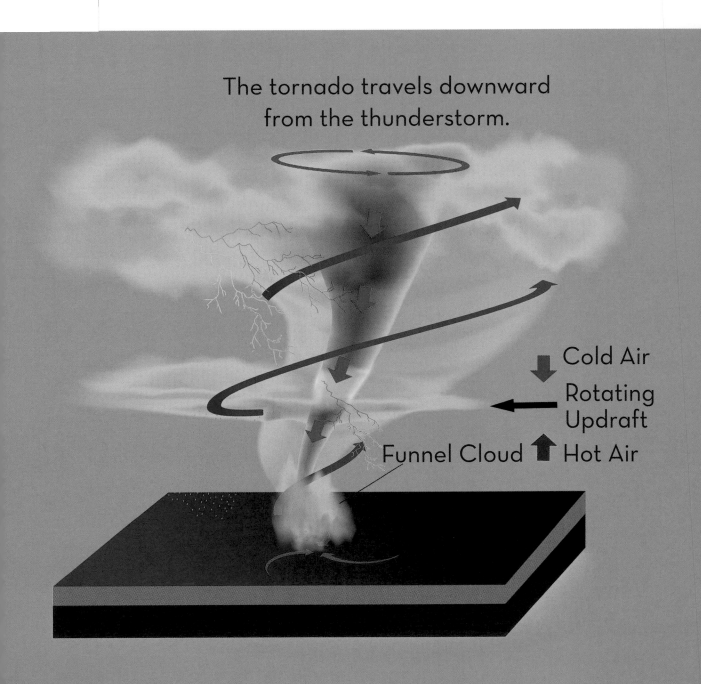

Cold Air

Rotating Updraft

Funnel Cloud | Hot Air

Tornadoes form when warm air and cold meet and begin to rotate.

Warm air usually rises. It is trapped under the heavier cold air. It cannot move upward. It begins to rotate. It creates a rotating **updraft**. The updraft gathers more warm air from the thunderstorm. Its rotation speed increases. Cold air is pushed beneath it. Water droplets in the updraft combine.

The droplets form a funnel cloud. The funnel descends from the storm and touches the ground. A tornado begins. Scientists aren't sure why some storms form tornadoes and others don't.

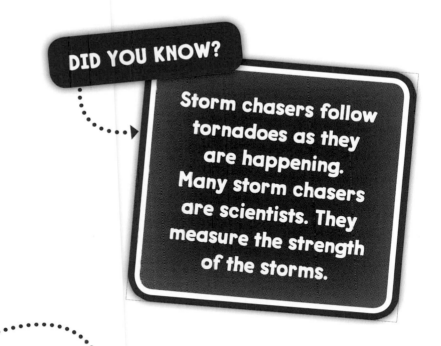

DID YOU KNOW?

Storm chasers follow tornadoes as they are happening. Many storm chasers are scientists. They measure the strength of the storms.

Most tornadoes form in the country, away from cities.

CHAPTER 4

What Kinds of Tornadoes Are There?

Tornadoes are produced by thunderstorms. Supercell tornadoes are the most common. The winds rotate very fast. The rotation is caused by a **wind shear**. Winds at two different points above the ground blow rapidly. They blow in different directions and sometimes at different speeds.

Supercell tornadoes can be very large and very dangerous.

Waterspouts are tornadoes that form over water.

Non-supercell tornadoes form when the wind rotates, but the clouds do not. They are usually small. The gustnado is a whirl of dust near the ground. A landspout has a funnel that looks like a rope. It has no rotating updraft. The spinning begins at ground level. It forms while a thunderstorm is developing. A waterspout is a weak tornado. It forms over warm water.

Tornadoes can cause a lot of damage.

Tornadoes can be very dangerous. Some are powerful enough to knock down trees or destroy buildings. The winds can carry dangerous **debris** that can injure people.

Meteorologists track tornadoes. They warn communities when a tornado is coming. They tell people to find shelter. Hiding underground or in basements is safest. Staying in sturdy buildings away from windows is also safe.

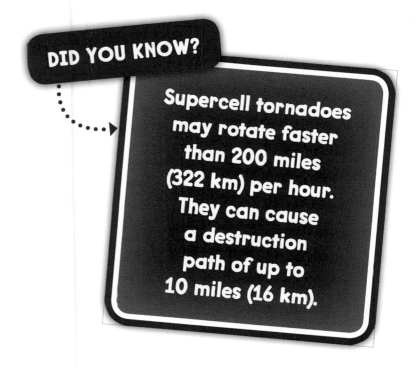

DID YOU KNOW?

Supercell tornadoes may rotate faster than 200 miles (322 km) per hour. They can cause a destruction path of up to 10 miles (16 km).

Glossary

atmosphere (AT-mos-feer) The atmosphere is made of the gasses surrounding the Earth and is often called air. Most tornadoes form in the spring and summer when the atmosphere is warm.

debris (duh-BREE) Debris is scattered pieces of objects caused by destruction. Broken windows may produce dangerous debris during a tornado.

dense (DENS) When particles or objects are packed closely together, they are dense. Cold air is more dense than warm air.

humid (HYOO-mid) Something that is humid is moist or damp. Humid air contains a lot of water vapor.

meteorologist (mee-tee-er-AWL-oh-jist) A meteorologist is a scientist who studies Earth's weather and atmosphere. Meteorologists try to predict rainstorms, snowstorms, and tornadoes.

updraft (UP-draft) An updraft is the upward movement of air or another gas. Rising warm air creates a tornado's updraft.

wind shear (WIND SHEER) A wind shear is a condition in which the speed or direction of wind changes abruptly. Wind shear can create a powerful updraft inside a tornado.

To Learn More

In the Library

Otfinoski, Steven. *Tornadoes*. New York, NY:
Children's Press, 2016.

Randolph, Joanne. *Tornado Alert!*
New York, NY: Enslow Publishing, 2018.

Ventura, Marne. *How to Survive a Tornado*.
Mankato, MN: The Child's World, 2016.

On the Web

Visit our website for links about tornadoes:
childsworld.com/links

Note to Parents, Teachers, and Librarians: We routinely verify our Web links to make sure they are safe and active sites. So encourage your readers to check them out!

Index